In Vietnam
En Vietnam

written by **Judy Zocchi** illustrated by **Neale Brodie**

dingles&company New Jersey

For Vincent Bianco

©2005 by Judith Mazzeo Zocchi

All rights reserved.
No part of this book may be reproduced in any form
without written permission from the publishers,
except by a reviewer who may quote brief passages
in a review to be printed in a newspaper or magazine.

First paperback printing

PUBLISHED BY dingles&company
P.O. Box 508 • Sea Girt, New Jersey • 08750
WEBSITE: www.dingles.com • E-MAIL: info@dingles.com

Library of Congress Catalog Card No.: 2004099334
ISBN: 1-59646-166-7

Printed in the United States of America

ART DIRECTION & DESIGN BY Barbie Lambert
ENGLISH EDITED BY Andrea Curley
SPANISH EDITED BY Teresa Carbajal Ravet
RESEARCH AND ADDITIONAL COPY WRITTEN BY Robert Neal Kanner
EDUCATIONAL CONSULTANT Bridget Riley Turnbach
PRE-PRESS BY Pixel Graphics

The Global Adventures series takes children on an around-the-world exploration of a variety of fascinating countries. The series examines each country's history and physical features as well as its most popular customs, activities, and foods.

Judy Zocchi

is the author of the Global Adventures, Holiday Happenings, Click & Squeak's Computer Basics, and Paulie and Sasha series. She is a writer and lyricist who holds a bachelor's degree in fine arts/theater from Mount Saint Mary's College and a master's degree in educational theater from New York University. She lives in Manasquan, New Jersey, with her husband, David.

Neale Brodie

is a freelance illustrator who lives in Brighton, England, with his wife and young daughter. He is a self-taught artist, having received no formal education in illustration. As well as illustrating a number of children's books, he has worked as an animator in the computer games industry.

In Vietnam a CYCLO is a bicycle taxi.

Once a common city vehicle, the slow-moving cyclo is now used only for transporting tourists.

En Vietnam un CICLO es un taxi de bicicleta.

Anteriormente un vehiculo común de la ciudad, el ciclo lento ahora se usa sólo para transportar a los turistas.

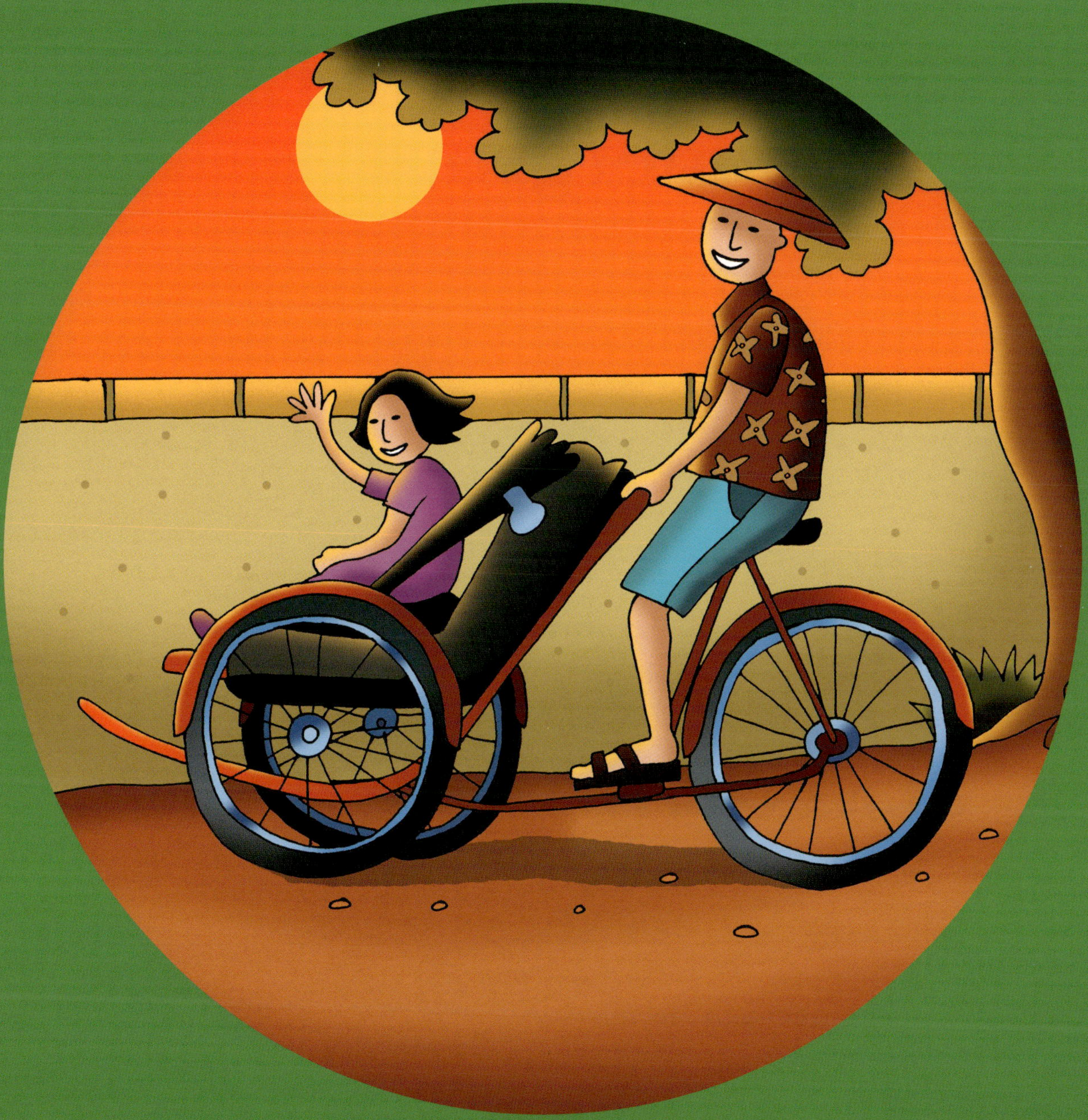

Tourists explore CU CHI TUNNELS underground.

Located in the Cu Chi district 25 miles northwest of Ho Chi Minh City is a vast network of connecting tunnels. During wars people used them to hide from military attacks. Today visitors can crawl through some of them.

Los turistas exploran los TÚNELES CU CHI subterráneos.

Situada en el distrito de Cu Chi a 40 km al noroeste de la Ciudad de Ho Chi Minh está una red vasta de túneles contiguos. Durante las guerras la gente los usaba para esconderse de los ataques militares. Ahora los turistas pueden gatear por algunos de ellos.

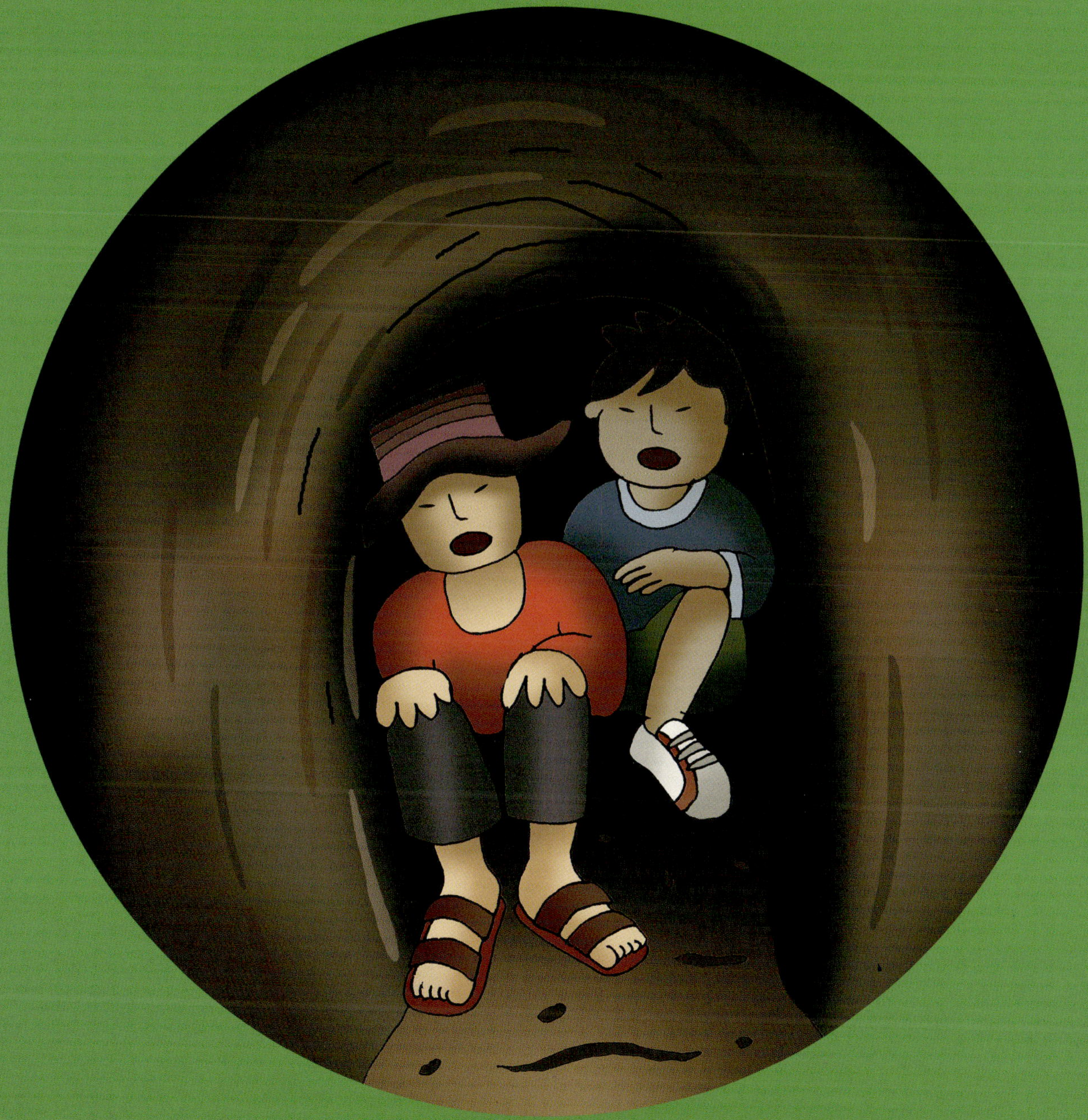

The DONG is what people spend.

The dong is the official currency of Vietnam.

El DONG es lo que la gente usa como moneda.

El dong es la moneda oficial de Vietnam.

500
CÔNG HÒA XÃ HỘI CHÙNGHA
VIỆT NAM
500
NĂM
TRĂM
ĐÔNG
500
CỘNG HÒA XÃ HỘI CHÙNGHĨA
NGAN HANG NHA NUOC VIETNAM
5000
DONG
10000
CÔNG HÒA XA HỘI CHỦ NGHĨA VIỆTNAM
10000
MUOI NGHIN DONG

Many people use MOTORCYCLES to get around.

People who live in and around Vietnam's crowded cities drive motorcycles or motorbikes because they are the fastest and easiest way to get through the narrow streets and crowded roads.

Mucha gente usa MOTOCICLETAS para movilizarse.

La gente quien vive en y por las ciudades de Vietnam conduce las motocicletas o las motonetas porque son las más rápidas y fáciles para manejar por las calles angostas y las carreteras ocupadas.

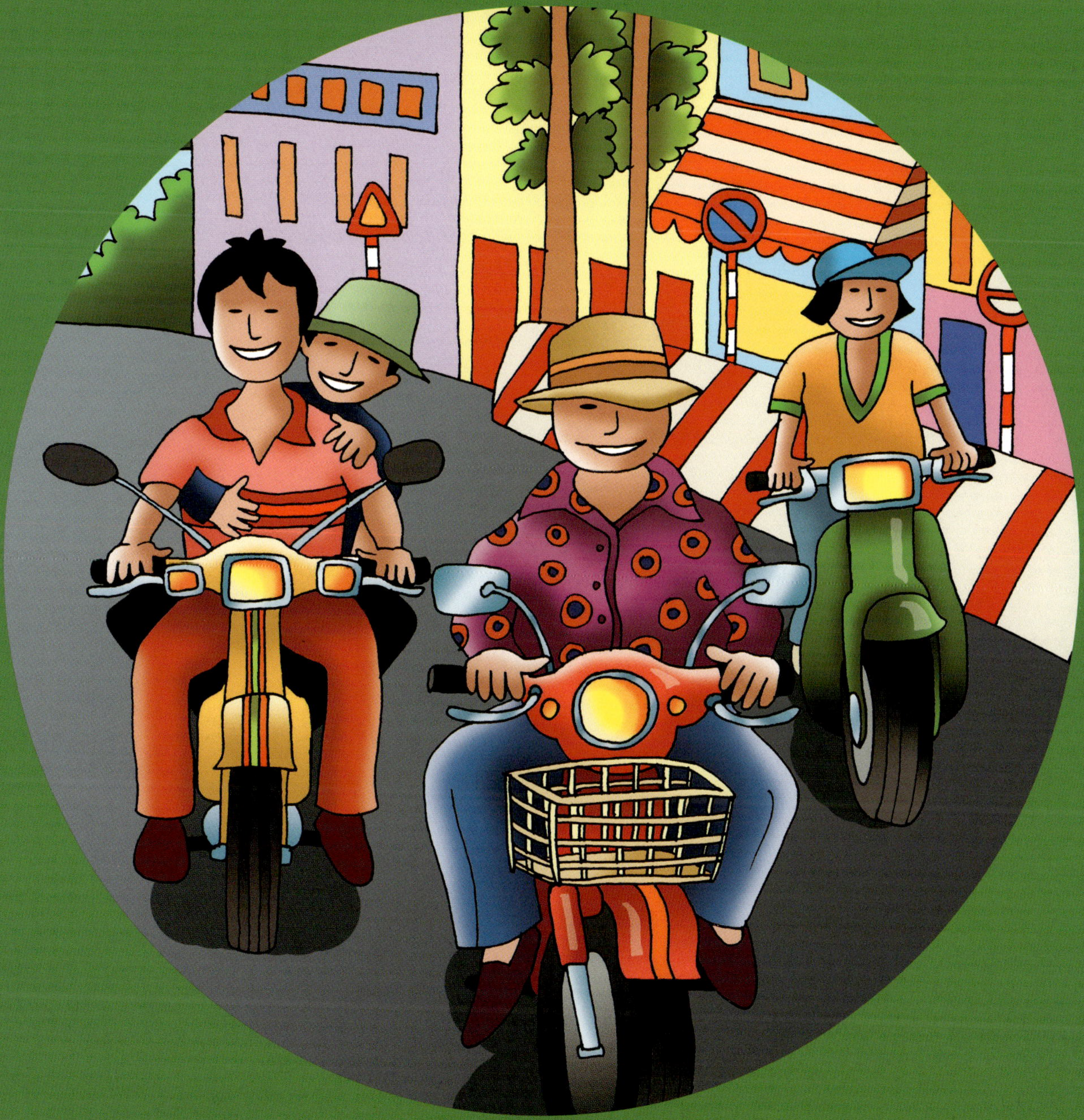

In Vietnam the DRAGON is a symbol of power.

According to legend, the Vietnamese are descendants of the dragon. The dragon can be seen in Vietnamese art dating back to prehistoric times. An image of the dragon appears on almost all pagodas, palaces, temples, tombs, and houses in the country.

En Vietnam el DRAGÓN es un símbolo de la potencia.

Según la leyenda, los vietnamitas son los descendientes del dragón. El dragón aparece en el arte vietnamés datando de tiempos prehistóricos. Una imagen del dragón aparece en casi todas las pagodas, los palacios, los templos, las tumbas, y las casas del país.

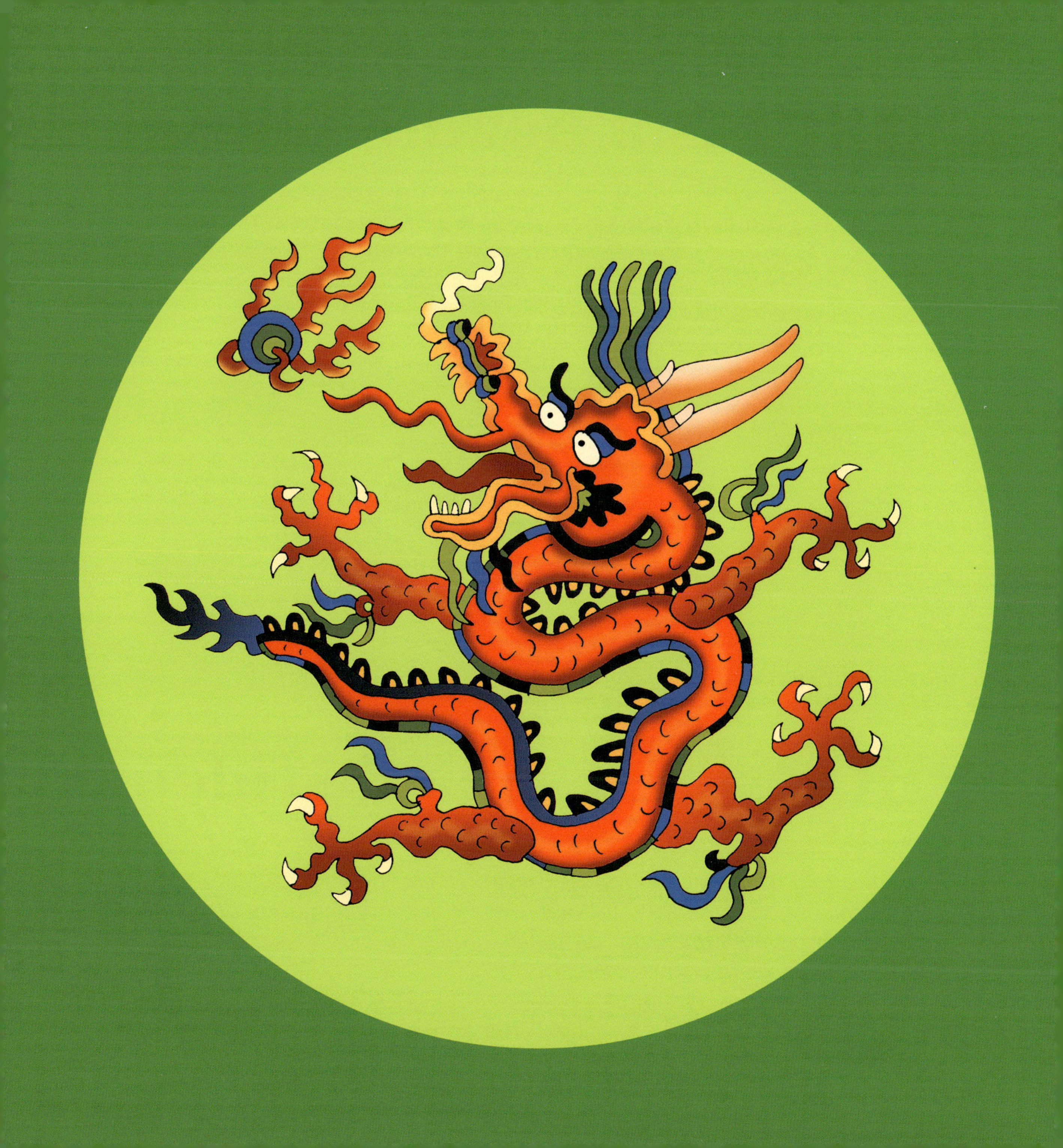

PHO is a noodle soup.

Pho is a common Vietnamese food. A well-seasoned steaming broth is poured over rice noodles and thin slices of raw beef or chicken. The diner stirs the noodles from the bottom of the bowl over the meat to cook it.

PHO es una sopa de fideos.

Pho es una comida común vietnamés. Un caldo bien sazonado y vaporoso se vierte sobre fideos de arroz y tajadas delgadas de carne cruda de res o pollo crudo. La persona mezcla los fideos del fondo del tazón sobre la carne para cocerla.

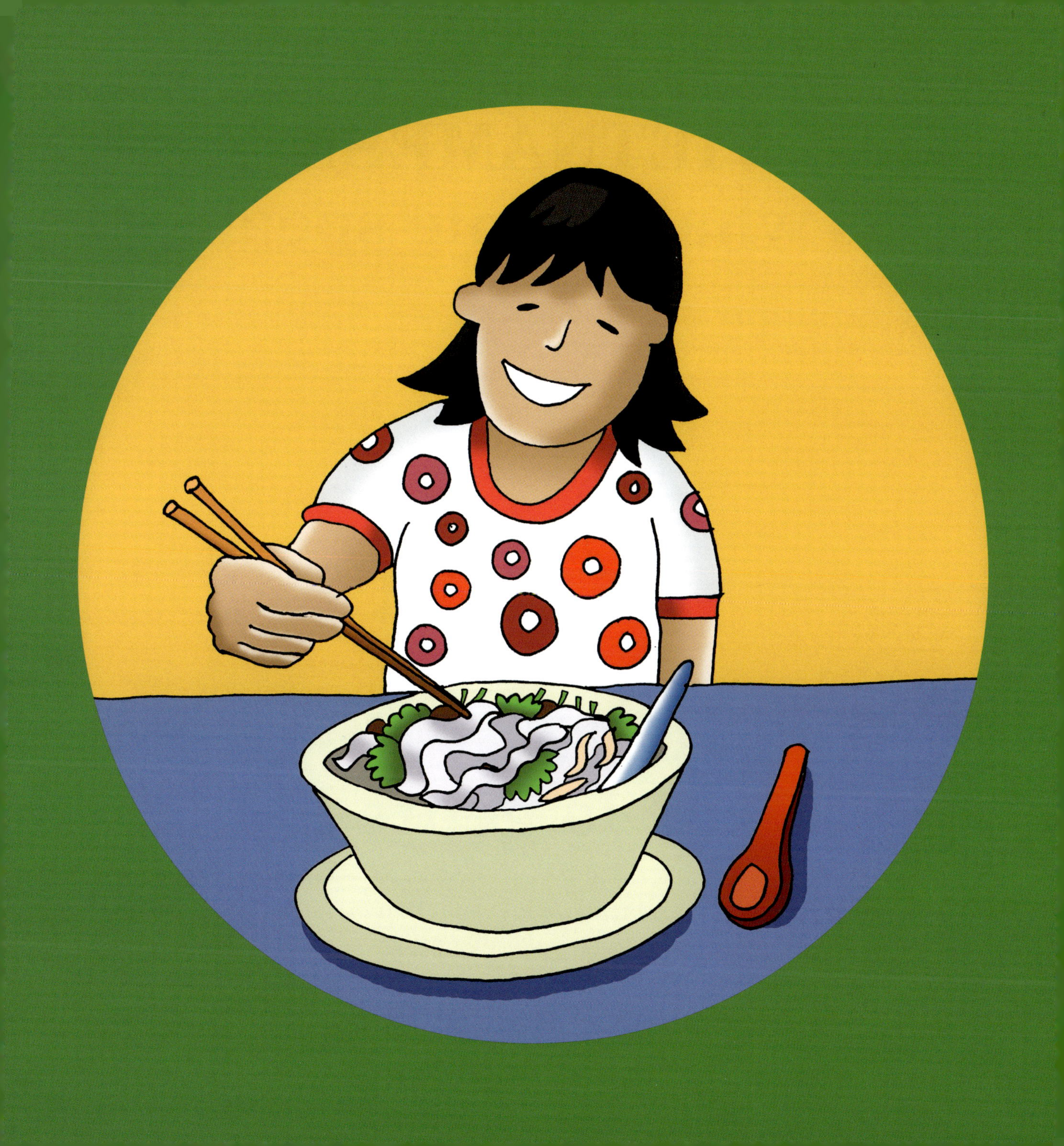

VIETNAMESE
is what people speak.

Vietnamese is the official language of Vietnam. It was originally written using Chinese characters but today uses the Latin alphabet.

VIETNAMÉS
es lo que la gente habla.

Vietnamés es el idioma oficial de Vietnam. Originalmente se escribía utilizando símbolos chinos pero ahora se utiliza el alfabeto latín.

I like this one. Me gusta éste.
I like the one over there. Me gusta aquél.

Puppeteers perform in a WATER PUPPETRY troupe.

In this ancient art form, puppeteers manipulate 2-foot-tall wooden puppets while standing in chest-deep pools of water. The puppeteers control the puppets by moving bamboo poles and strings that are hidden by backdrops and water.

Titiriteros representan en una compañía TEATRAL ACUÁTICA de títeres.

En esta forma antigua de arte, los titiriteros manipulan los títeres de madera de 61 cm de altura mientras están dentro de piscinas de agua, llenas hasta el pecho. Los titiriteros controlan los títeres por manipular postes de bambú y cuerdas que están escondidos por telones de fondo y agua.

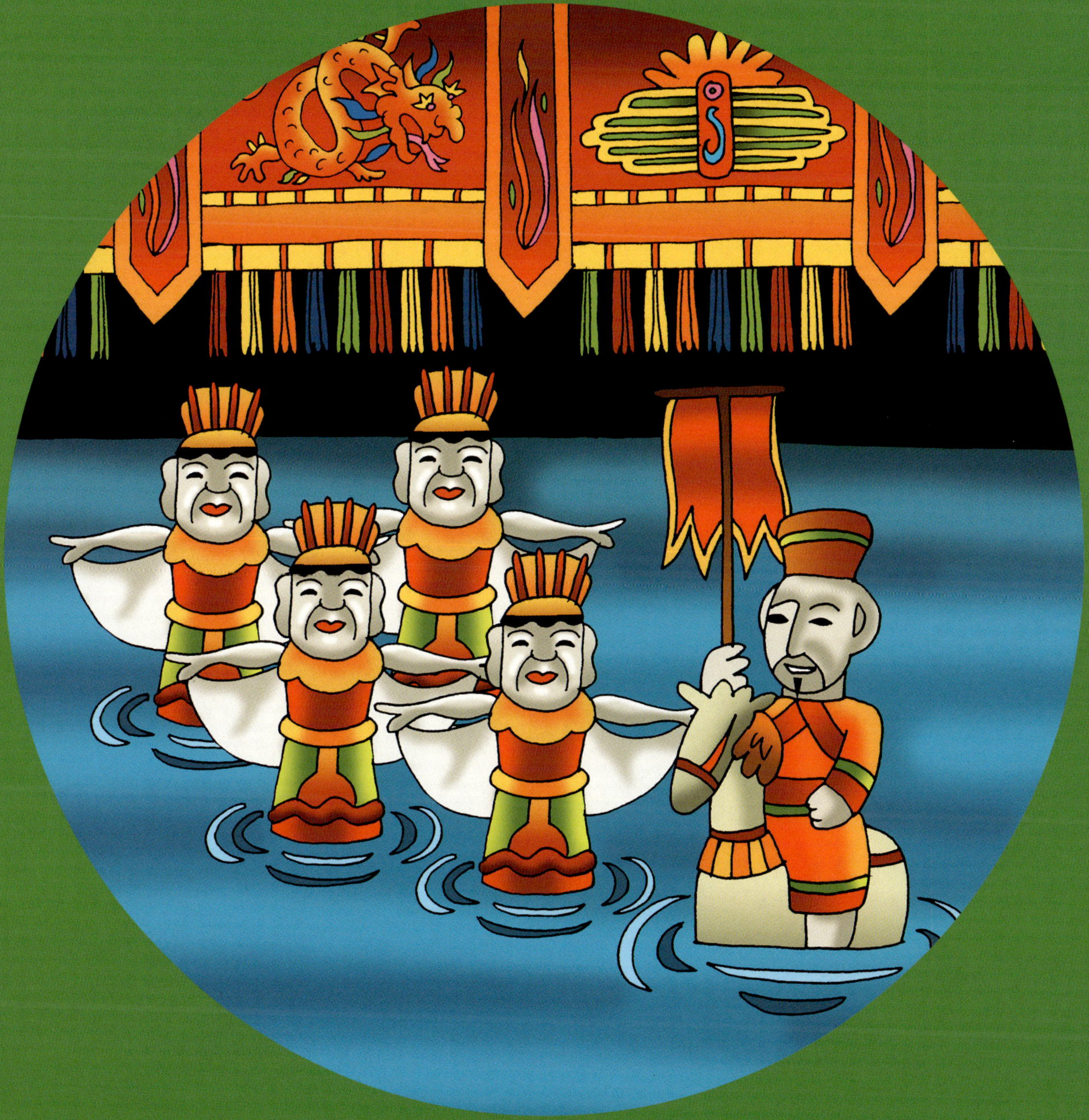

In Vietnam people gather at daily FISH MARKETS.

Fishing is an important industry because seafood is plentiful along Vietnam's very long coastline. There are always crowds of people buying and selling fish in the early morning hours at Vietnam's world famous fish markets.

En Vietnam la gente se reúne diariamente en los MERCADOS DE PECES.

La pesca es una industria importante porque el marisco es abundante a lo largo de la costa de Vietnam. Siempre hay masas de gente comprando y vendiendo pescado temprano durante las horas de la mañana en los mercados de peces de fama mundial.

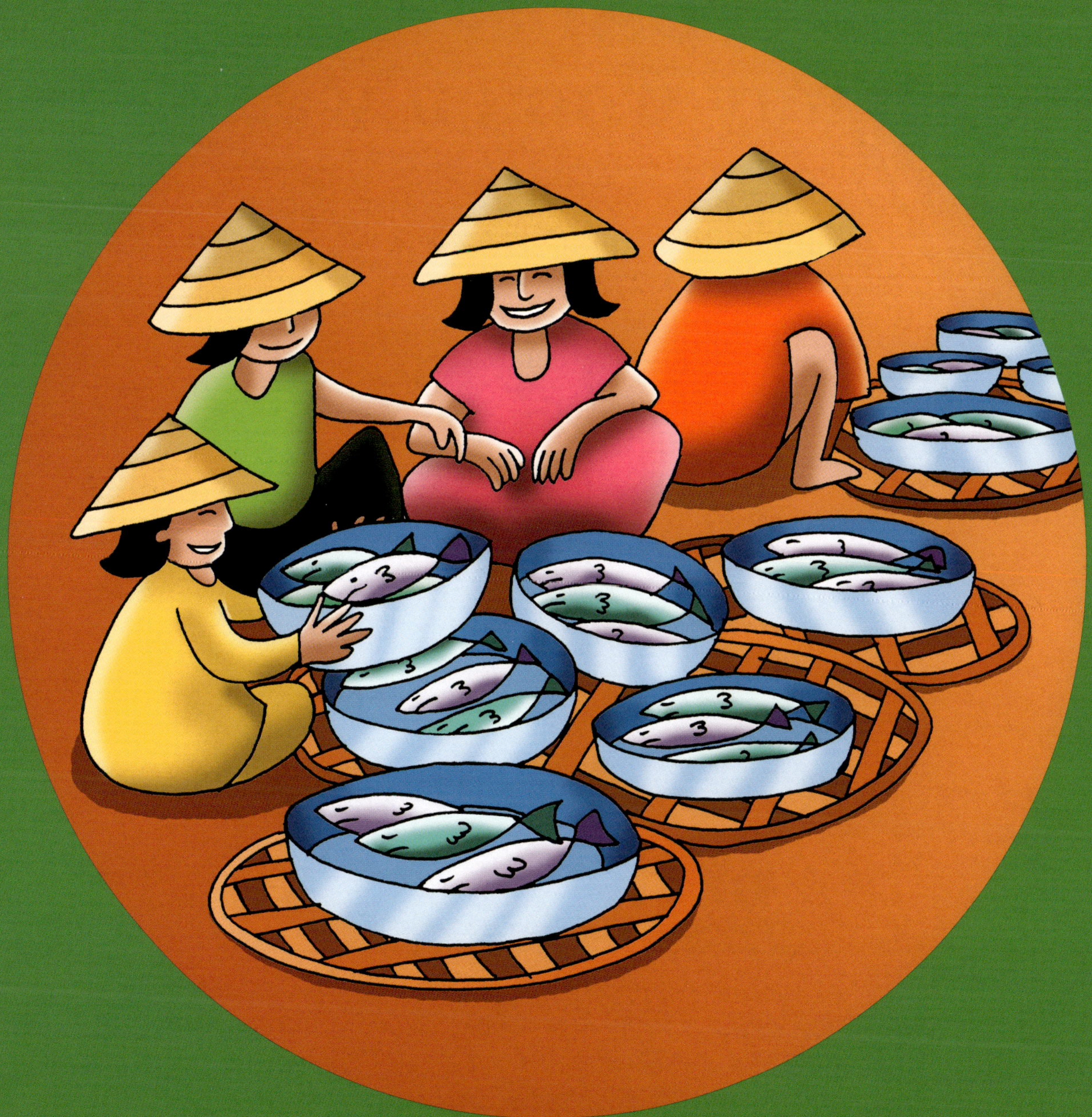

AO DAI is what many women wear.

This is the traditional dress for women. It consists of long, loose trousers worn under a long-sleeved, tight-fitting tunic with slits on both sides.

AO DAI es lo que las mujeres llevan.

Este es el vestido tradicional para las mujeres. Consiste de pantalones largos y flojos llevados de bajo de una túnica ajustada de mangas largas y cortes en ambos lados.

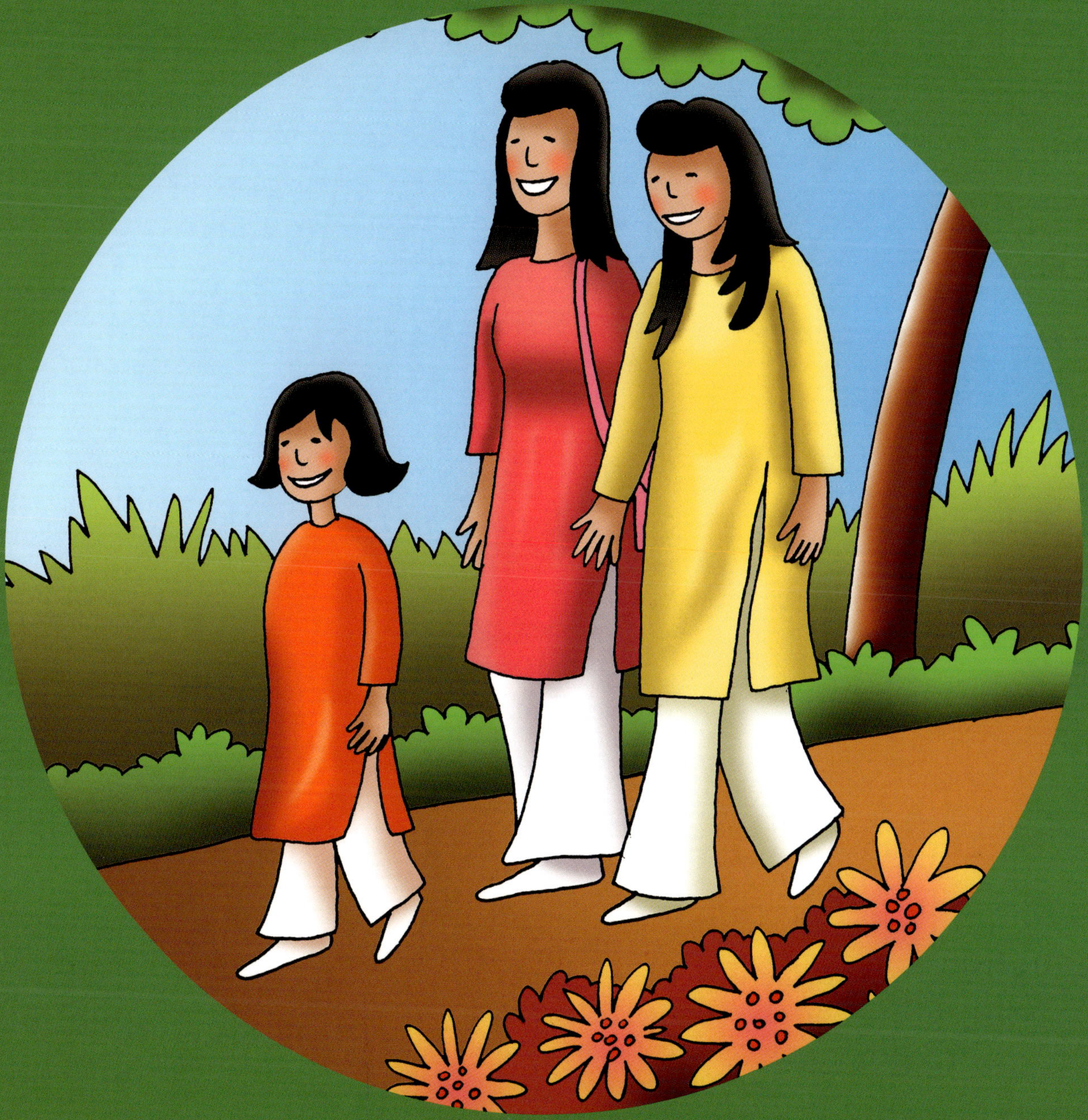

The JAVAN RHINOCEROS is at risk.

This large, one-horned rhino was widespread and abundant throughout Southeast Asia but is now an endangered species. Today there are only two known populations, totaling less than sixty animals. They live in reserves in Java, Indonesia, and Vietnam.

El RINOCERONTE JAVAN está en peligro.

Este rinoceronte grande y mogón fue difundido y abundante a través Asia Sudoriental pero ahora es una especie en peligro de extinción. Actualmente sólo hay dos poblaciones conocidas, de suma total de menos de sesenta animales. Viven en una reserva en Java, Indonesia, y Vietnam.

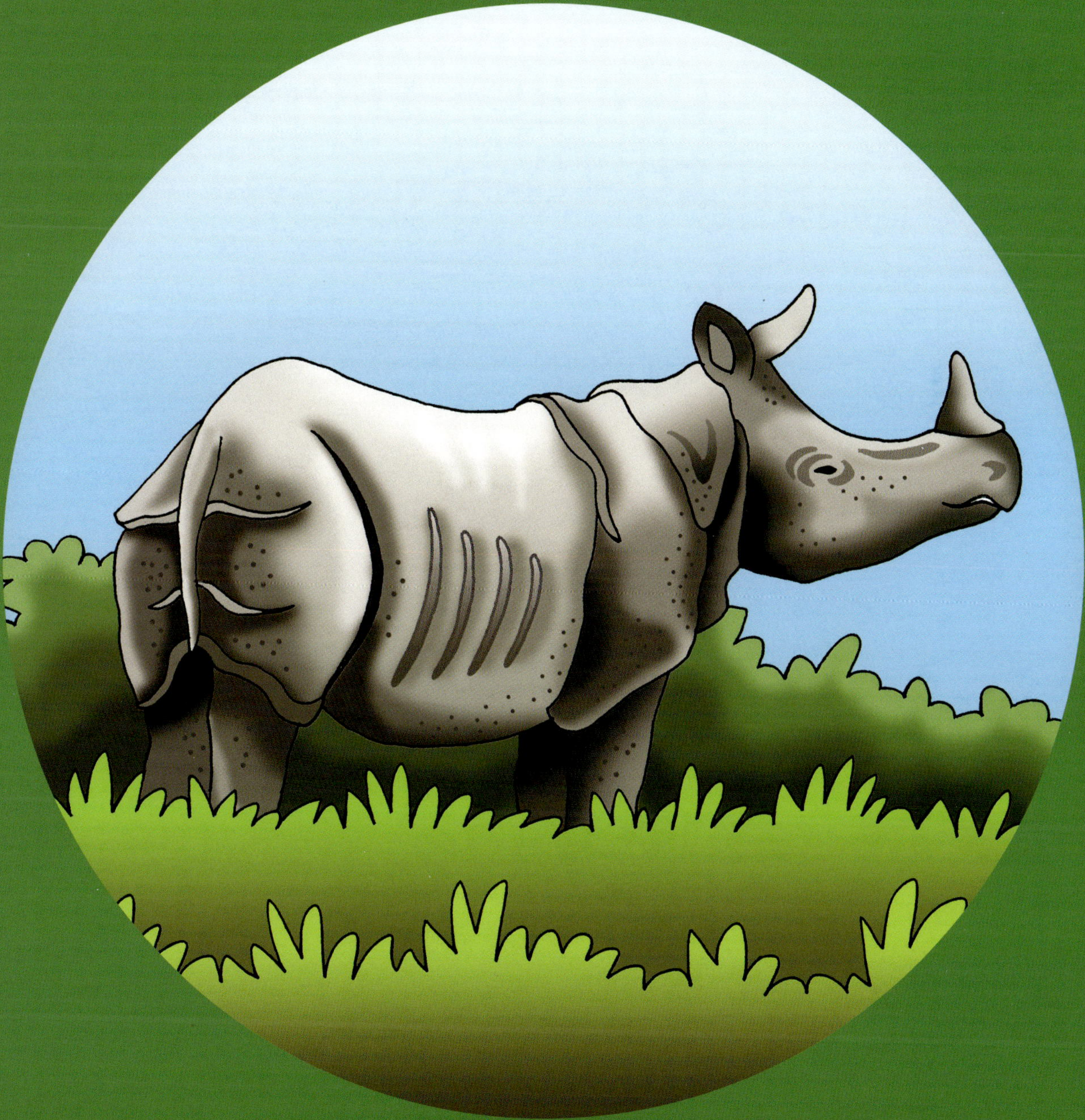

BASKET BOATS help people get from here to there.

Many coastal villagers, both children and adults, fish using these small, round, woven-bamboo boats.

BOTES DE CESTA ayudan a la gente a movilizarse de aquí para allá.

Muchos aldeanos costeros, niños y adultos, pescan utilizando estos botes pequeños, redondos, y tejidos de bambú.

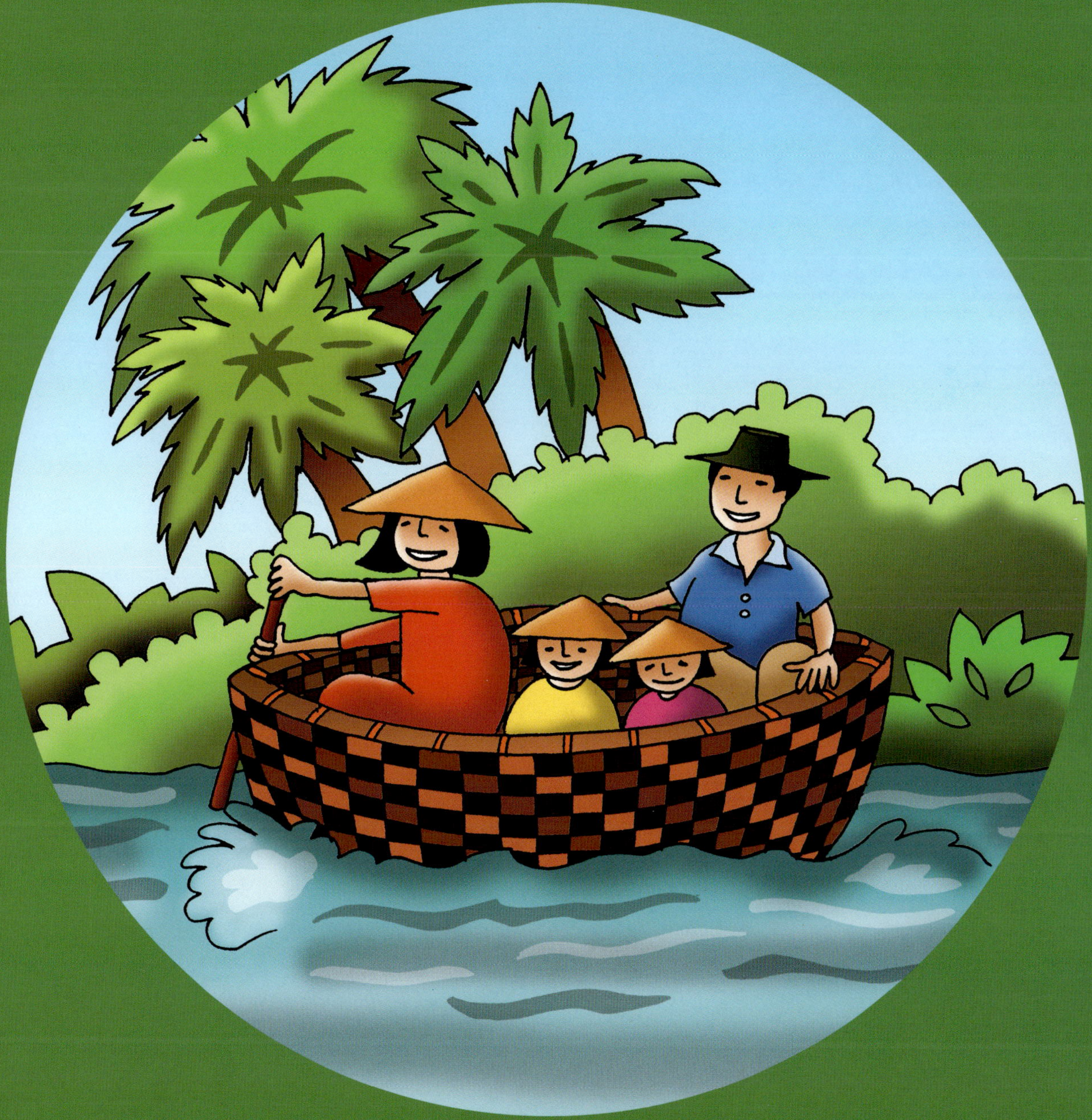

Vietnamese culture is fun to learn.

La cultura Vietnamés es divertida para aprender.

CYCLO
(SEE-clo)

CU CHI TUNNELS
(CU-chee)

DONG
(DOM)

MOTORCYCLES

DRAGON

PHO
(FUH)

VIETNAMESE

WATER PUPPETRY

FISH MARKETS

AO DAI
(OW-zhie)

JAVAN RHINOCEROS

BASKET BOATS

VIETNAM

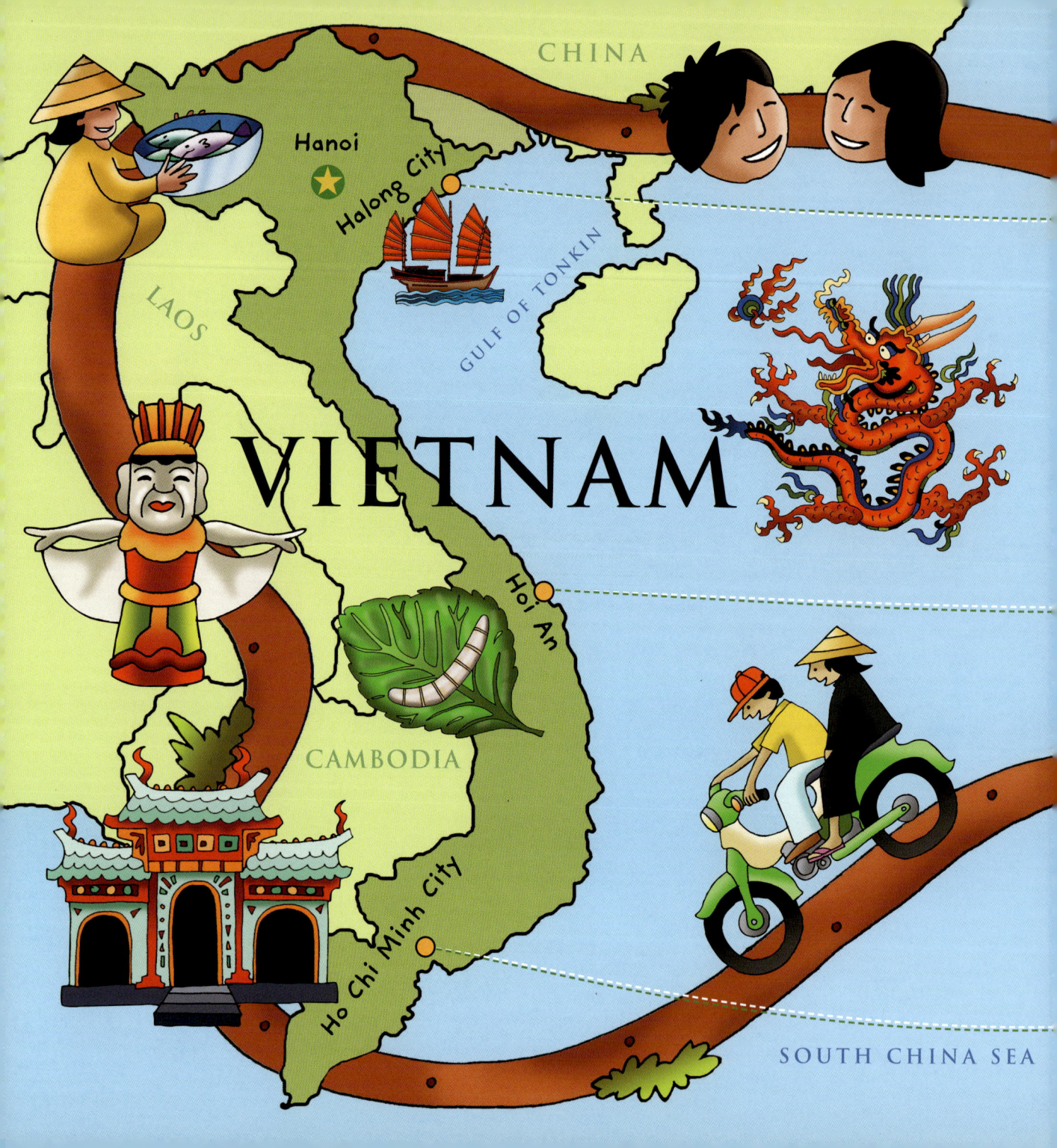

CHINA

Hanoi

Halong City

GULF OF TONKIN

LAOS

Hoi An

CAMBODIA

Ho Chi Minh City

SOUTH CHINA SEA

Halong City: Hire a boat and explore beautiful Halong Bay, with its 3,000 islands, fjords, and inlets.

Ciudad Halong: Alquila un bote y explora la bella Bahía Halong, con sus 3.000 islas, fiordos y ensenadas.

Hoi An: This port city is famous for its silk fabric. At some shops you can see silkworms at work, making silk!

Hoi An: Esta ciudad portuaria es famosa por su tela de seda. En algunas tiendas puedes ver a los gusanos de seda trabajando, ¡haciendo seda!

Ho Chi Minh City: At the Ong Bon Pagoda, people burn fake paper money, hoping that the god Ong Bon will bring them wealth in the coming year.

Ciudad Ho Chi Minh: En el Pagoda Ong Bon, la gente quema moneda falsa de papel con la esperanza de que el dios Ong Bon le traiga riqueza para el año que viene.

See what you can discover at every turn!

•

Mira qué puedes descubrir por cada vuelta.

OFFICIAL NAME:
Socialist Republic of Vietnam

CAPITAL CITY:
Hanoi

CURRENCY:
Dong

MAJOR LANGUAGE:
Vietnamese

BORDERS:
China, Gulf of Tonkin, South China Sea, Laos, Cambodia

CONTINENT:
Asia

ABOUT VIETNAM

An ancient Viet race lived in the area now known as Vietnam. China conquered the northern area in 111 B.C.E. and ruled over it for more than 1,000 years. A Viet people in the south finally defeated the Chinese and ended their rule. Many different Viet empires controlled the area until the French claimed the land as their own in the late 1800s. In 1954 the French were forced to leave by a group known as the Viet Minh. They were communists who believed that the government should own and control the land and businesses. The country was divided. The communists, led by Ho Chi Minh, occupied the north. The nationalists lived in the south. They created a democratic government in which the people could vote for government officials and own land and businesses. In 1963, the communist tried to take over the south. This was the start of what became known as the Vietnam War. The United States entered the war to help the southern nationalists. In 1975, after many years of war, North Vietnamese forces captured South Vietnam's capital city, Saigon, and the south surrendered. This ended the war and reunified the country under communist control. Today, the communists still control Vietnam. Much of the country is mountainous and hilly, with rice paddies in the coastal areas. Painting on silk, puppetry, and ceramics are popular crafts. The major industries are rice, rubber, and tourism.

UNDERSTANDING AND CELEBRATING CULTURAL DIFFERENCES

- What do you have in common with children from Vietnam?
- What things do you do differently from the children in Vietnam?
- What is your favorite new thing you learned about Vietnam?
- What unique thing about your culture would you like to share?

TRAVELING THROUGH VIETNAM

- On which coast of the southeast Asian peninsula does Vietnam lie?
- In which direction would you be traveling if you went from Hanoi to Ho Chi Minh City?
- Into which sea does the Mekong River flow?

TRY SOMETHING NEW...

Make a dan day (a traditional Vietnamese lute) by tying three pieces of plastic string around any hollow container. Use your fingers to play music for your family and friends!

For more information on the Global Adventures series or to find activities that coordinate with it, explore our website at **www.dingles.com**.